Contents

On the move

Look up!

It's a helicopter!

It can fly up and down.

It can fly left and right.

It can spin.

It can hover too.

It stays in one place in the air.

Parts

Look at the rotor

blades. They spin fast.

Time to fly!

Here is the cockpit.

It has levers and pedals.

Pilots use them to fly.

pedal

lever

13

Look at the the skids.

A helicopter lands on them.

skids

Types

A helicopter can carry water.

It puts out fires.

A helicopter can carry cameras.

It helps to show the news.

camera

A helicopter can carry people.

Look at the big city!

Glossary

blade   one of the long, flat parts of a helicopter's rotor

cockpit   place where the pilot sits in a helicopter

hover   stay in one place in the air

lever   bar that is used to make a machine or vehicle work

pedal   flat part that you push with your foot to make a machine work

pilot   person who flies a helicopter or aeroplane

rotor   set of rotating blades that lifts an aircraft off the ground

skid   one of a pair of long narrow parts on the bottom of a helicopter or aeroplane; some helicopters land on skids

Find out more

Books

Big Machines Fly! (Big Machines), Catherine Veitch (Raintree, 2015)

Getting Around Through the Years: How Transport has Changed in Living Memory (History in Living Memory), Clare Lewis (Raintree, 2016)

Look Inside Things That Go (Usborne Look Inside) Rob Lloyd Jones (Usborne Publishing Ltd, 2013)

True or False? Transport, Dan Nunn (Raintree, 2014)

Websites

www.dkfindout.com/uk/transport/history-aircraft/helicopters/
Learn the history of helicopters.

http://www.bbc.co.uk/education/clips/zcnhgk7
Learn how a ranch in Australia uses helicopters to round up cattle.

Comprehension questions

1. How is a helicopter different from an aeroplane?

2. Name two ways that helicopters can help people.

3. What parts do helicopters use to fly?

Index